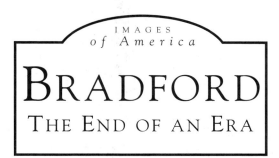

IMAGES
of America

BRADFORD
THE END OF AN ERA

The First Church of Christ's 1853 "White Church." This is the fifth meetinghouse built for Bradford's first parish. The first two buildings were on Salem Street with the old Burial Ground. The third was on the Common, and the fourth and fifth were on Church Street facing the Common. Henry Ford so admired the design that he asked for, and received, permission to copy it for his four Martha and Mary chapels, including the one at Greenfield Village, Michigan. The vestry, the small building to the right was later moved to Laurel Avenue where it served as a primary school.

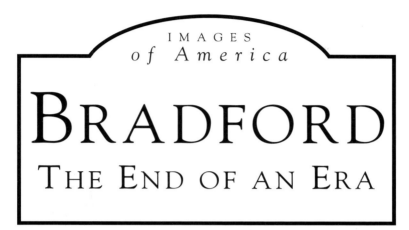

IMAGES
of America

BRADFORD
THE END OF AN ERA

*To Nomi,
with appreciation for all your cooperation
in this project!*

Patricia Trainor O'Malley

Patricia T. O'Malley

ARCADIA

First published 1996
Copyright © Patricia Trainor O'Malley, 1996

ISBN 0-7524-0426-1

Published by Arcadia Publishing,
an imprint of the Chalford Publishing Corporation
One Washington Center, Dover, New Hampshire 03820
Printed in Great Britain

Library of Congress Cataloging-in-Publication Data applied for

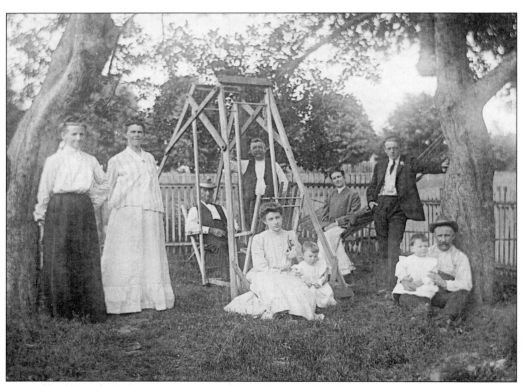

A Bradford Family Relaxes on a Spring Day. Their backyard seems to be equipped with the latest in lawn swings.

Cover Image: The Carleton School for Boys and Young Men, 286 South Main Street, 1884–1902.

Contents

Bradford Academy Student Photographers. The development of the simple box camera by George Eastman in the late 1880s made photography America's most democratic art, and its ability to capture everyday life gives us a rare glimpse into the past. Many of the photographs in this volume were taken by these young camera enthusiasts from Bradford Academy.

Introduction

Bradford, Massachusetts, has been a part of the city of Haverhill since January 1, 1897. The two face each other across the swiftly flowing Merrimack River, Bradford on the south bank and Haverhill on the north. There is a northerly curve in the river where the Main Street links the two, and on a map it appears that Bradford fits right into Haverhill, like a ball in a glove. But this part of the city is never called South Haverhill, nor are there many who live there who identify themselves as being from Haverhill. Bradford is their home, and Bradford is their identity. And behind that statement is a story. And it begins, "Once upon a time . . ."

Once upon a time, Bradford was an independent town. In truth, it had been an independent town from very early on in the history of Massachusetts. By 1670, a sufficient number of families lived there for it to earn its own meetinghouse. Independence from the mother colony of Rowley was not long in coming. Bradford was an agricultural town through the eighteenth century, with farms dotted along the Merrimack beyond the neck of land across from Methuen. But progress was pulling Bradford closer to Haverhill. First, a new meetinghouse was built further west along Salem Street near to where the ferry crossed the river. Soon a Common was set out and merchants and shoe makers began to build their homes nearby. In 1794, a bridge was built to replace the ferry, and because Haverhill was more advantageously sited for shipping, commerce became concentrated on that side of the river. Then, when the Boston & Maine Railroad decided to establish a line through Bradford and Haverhill toward Portland, Maine, the die was cast. The new brick factory buildings for the infant shoe industry would be built in Haverhill, and Bradford would increasingly become a residence for those who made a living across the river.

In 1850, the eastern half of Bradford separated to form the new town of Groveland and this concentrated Bradford's population even more toward downtown Haverhill. When Haverhill became a city in 1870, the call for annexation began to be heard. The call would be repeated for the next twenty-five years without either location able to agree as the vote flip-flopped in election after election. The call was finally heard, and listened to, in 1896, and this time the first move came from Bradford. The rest, as they say, is history.

People voted for annexation for a variety of reasons. Finances played a large part. Those with businesses in Haverhill and homes in Bradford wanted more say in Haverhill's government. Prohibitionists looked at Bradford's long tradition of voting "dry" and wanted to add those votes to their supporters in Haverhill so that the city would become "dry." Much liquor money poured into the city prior to the election. Liquor dealers in Portsmouth, New Hampshire, funded a great deal of newspaper advertising against annexation (and in support of their interests). However, liquor dealers in nearby Lawrence, Massachusetts, poured almost as much money into advertising in favor of annexation, on the presumption that a "dry" Haverhill would encourage drinkers to go to Lawrence for their liquor.

The demand for municipal services, a large budget item in Haverhill, persuaded many from Bradford to support annexation. The development of Ward Hill in Bradford's southernmost area, miles from downtown Bradford, had led to repeated calls to extend town services to that part of town, a project that the conservative town meeting was reluctant to undertake. Residents of Ward Hill would be among the leaders of the annexation movement.

Haverhill had a new library, new hospital, new schools, a new downtown factory area, and "new" was in style. Bradford seemed conservative, old-fashioned, and not up-to-date, especially to the increasing number of newcomers to the town.

Annexation was also about ethnic minorities. Bradford was mostly "Yankee" with a small minority of Irish and French Canadians. Haverhill had far more of the same, but also a rapidly growing population of "new" immigrants from southern and eastern Europe. There were many insinuations in the press, and in private, about what would happen to Haverhill if this infusion of immigrants continued. Adding Bradford's Yankee population to Haverhill's would keep power in the "proper" hands.

The reasons, many and varied, have become difficult to interpret after all these years. However, it is apparent that, the more time that has passed since 1896, the greater the nostalgia for what once was. The "idea" of Bradford endures.

Bradford is also a school. Once Bradford Academy, now Bradford College, it rests its solid weight high on a hill in the center of town. Its presence since 1803 has given a special quality to its locale, and along with the Common, the white-spired church, and the surrounding stately houses, it brings to mind the images of a "typical New England town." The Academy then, as the College does now, brought international recognition to the town.

In this, the centennial year of Bradford's loss of independence, we offer a look at those long-ago days. We have created a pictorial tour of the town beginning at the riverfront and ending at Ward Hill. The people and places of a hundred years ago are here. The photographs range from formal shots taken by professionals to quick snapshots taken by family and friends. The quality is not always the best, but the personal tone offsets any technical problems. Because houses were a favorite topic of the photographers, we have chosen to include information on architectural styles. In effect, then, this book can also serve as a guide to the architectural history of Bradford. Most of the photographs date from the 1890s and early 1900s.

The addresses given are those used in the present. Bradford streets, which replicated names already in Haverhill, had "South" attached to them in the 1920s. Some street names have been changed, and we have tried to indicate this wherever necessary.

This is not intended to be a thorough survey of Bradford. Many leading figures are not shown, but that reflects the nature of the sources, not some editorial decision. Instead, what we offer is an introduction to the richness of the collections of two local libraries, supplemented by a handful of pictures from private sources.

Many of the photographs come from the incredible pictorial archive at the Haverhill Public Library. Most of the rest come from the Bradfordiana archive at the College. Because the new candid camera caught on very quickly among the Academy students, and because many of their photo albums have been left to the College's archives, we are able to offer many informal shots that help to give life to the past. A number of the photographs at the College were in a short-lived process called cyanotype, which produced a blue-tinted picture on a thin, uncoated paper. Other long-forgotten photograph processes that we have used include glass plates, tintypes, and *carte de visites*. A number of photographs are of the Donovan family. They are part of a treasure trove of family memorabilia that deserve a book all their own.

This book would have been impossible without the cheerful cooperation of the two libraries. To the Trustees of the Haverhill Public Library, to former Director Howard Curtis now far off in California, and to Greg Laing of the Special Collections, many thanks for the hours of help, advice, information, and wisdom. And to Ruth Hooten, librarian of Bradford College, and Nancy Pedersen, archivist for Bradfordiana, thanks for opening up all those treasures to me! I've had the pleasure of taking enlargements of some of these Bradford pictures out "on the road" to meetings with Bradford Alumni, and I hope we can inspire others to contribute their photographs to the archives. My gratitude also to my neighbor and former student, Steve Sardella, for sharing his Ward Hill and Thornton family photographs with me, and to Polly Roberts for her Horne family photograph. Finally, a very special thank you to my mother, Marie Donovan Trainor, born in Bradford in 1903, soon after annexation, who has shared with us her Donovan family photographs and other artifacts, along with her love for her hometown.

This one's for you, Mike.

One
From the Bridge
to Central Square

The Tie That Binds. The bridge to Haverhill connected South Main Street in Bradford with Main Street in Haverhill. Above, Bradford fire engines race across the bridge to assist their neighbors. The driver of the first engine (Hose #5) is Sidney Mason, the town's first African-American fireman. The date of the photograph is c. 1897.

On the Way to Haverhill, 1897. Carolyn Hazard poses on the bridge with her camera.

Academy Girls on a Saturday Shopping Trip. Academy rules allowed visiting in Haverhill only on Saturdays, and the girls were required to walk with a companion.

A Spring Flood under the Bridge. A curious crowd gathers to watch the Merrimack River fill its banks to overflowing. This bridge was built in 1870. It was replaced in 1925 by the present Basiliere Bridge.

The N. Brittain & Co. Meat Market at the Bridge. The steps down to the Haverhill Bridge Depot were directly beneath the sign advertising "Cigars And Tobacco."

The Haverhill Bridge Depot. This station on the Bradford side of the river serviced the branch of the Boston & Maine Railroad to Georgetown.

The Hotel Bradford, 31 South Main Street. The building on the right had a short life as a hotel and livery stable (1894–1897). The woman walking past the hotel was Mlle. Elisa Meyer, language instructor at the Academy. A student's wish to capture her teacher on film has also preserved this rare view of the hotel for future generations.

Working-Class Homes. This cluster of four-and-a-half-story mansard-roofed houses is on River Street in Bradford, beside the branch line of the railroad.

The South Kimball Street School. Opened in 1903, this was one of the rare wooden school buildings still in use in the mid-1900s. The land from the river to the Common had belonged to the Kimballs in the early years of the town, and the street and school bear that family's name.

The Haverhill Boxboards Company, South Kimball Street. This business (formerly the Haverhill Paper Company) and the Gilman Hat Company, a mile west on the river, were the only industrial buildings in downtown Bradford.

Boxboards Workers. The lower end of Bradford, between the river and Doane Street, east of South Main Street, was a highly built up area of multi-family homes, many of them occupied by recent immigrants. The Boxboards was a primary employer of many of these people whose days, like those of most of Bradford's residents, were marked by twice-daily blasts of the Boxboards' whistle.

Central Square, *c.* 1900. Bradford's business district, from the bridge to Doane and Carleton Streets, was still a mix of old homes, homes converted to businesses on the first floor, and newer mercantile blocks. This is the junction of South Main and South Pleasant Streets, looking south toward the Common and the Academy.

The Intersection of South Main and South Pleasant Streets. This time, the photographer was looking north, from the opposite side of South Pleasant Street.

Central Square. This, and the following three pictures, are of the same location, looking north toward Haverhill, along South Main Street from the South Pleasant Street intersection. The trolley tracks and the clothing styles date this photograph from the late nineteenth century.

Snowdrifts in Central Square. These drifts reached up to the first floor of some of the buildings. Snow removal was not a priority!

A Closer View in Much More Pleasant Weather. Note the summer dresses on the women to the left and the awnings on the storefronts. The house on the right belonged to the Payson family and the small shop in front of it served as the post office from 1887 to 1898. It later years, it would be a grocery store, a barber shop, and an antiques business. The space is now occupied by a car dealership.

The Co-operative Store at the Junction of South Main and Ferry Streets, c. 1916. This shop, located on the site of the former post office, was an early version of the small chain stores like the A&P and The First National that would soon appear to compete with family stores.

The Bradford Market, 67–69 South Main Street. Originally, this was the home of Reverend Jonathan Allen, minister of the First Church at the beginning of the nineteenth century. The structure was formerly located across from Bradford Academy where Allen Street is today. The two-story house was probably placed atop the street-level stores when it was moved to the South Main Street site.

Interior, Bradford Market, 1914. Behind the counter are Phil Primack, Alfonso Nesbitt, an unidentified man, and Maury Lewis (the driver for the market).

The Eliot House, 80 South Main Street. This was a simple two-bay eighteenth-century house. The picket fence was a popular mid-1800s addition and represented a new trend toward privacy. This is a 1916 photograph, though the barefoot boy could be equally at home fifty years earlier.

The Dr. George E. Allen House. This house was originally the Tenney family house, located at the corner of South Central at South Main Streets. It was built in the 1830s, but its design is the earlier Adam, or Federal, style. Both the Eliot and Allen Houses, as well as the neighboring houses in both pictures, have been razed.

South Pleasant Street from South Summer Street, c. 1895. Many of the homes have Greek Revival styling, suggesting they were built in the second quarter of the nineteenth century. Here, too, fenced-in yards were very popular.

James and Margaret Donovan. Father and daughter are sitting on the front "stoop" of their house at 10 South Pleasant Street. Jim died of the "white plague," that is, tuberculosis, shortly after this photograph was taken. Tuberculosis was the leading killer of that era.

Two Young Women Pause on South Main Street near Carleton Avenue. The small house behind them was the home of Johnny "Gee, Jumbo!" Roche, an early Irish immigrant who died in 1911 at the age of ninety-two. Johnny kept a cow, with the incongruous name of "Pig Mary," behind the house.

Carlisle & Holt, the Principal Grocery Store in Bradford from 1908 until 1950. The handsome brick building, built originally for Frederick Johnson early in the nineteenth century for his West Indies goods store, has since served as an undertaker's parlor, Maguire's Bradford Store, and professional offices.

Ferry Street. The large elegant houses, tall trees, and cobblestoned street of the nineteenth century bear little resemblance to today's street with its shopping strip mall and auto dealership. The name of the street is a reminder from centuries past that this was the way to the river crossing before the first bridge was put up in 1794.

The Leonard Johnson House on Ferry Street, just off of Central Square. Built in 1854 in the Italianate style, the building was razed in 1955 to make way for a shopping plaza. This photograph was taken in the 1870s. The house contained Bradford's first combination bathtub and shower, an elaborate copper unit.

Leonard Johnson (1798–1865), the Brother of Frederick Johnson (p. 31). Leonard was a shoe manufacturer and a trustee of Bradford Academy from 1832 to 1865.

The David Kimball House, 13 Ferry Street. This brick Federal-style house with a hip roof was built about 1825, when David Kimball (1795–1873) was married. It is a mate to that built by his brother George on Salem Street (p. 47). This photograph was taken about 1890, when the house was occupied by F.R. Trask. The building now houses Costello's Insurance Company.

An Independent Ice Company Wagon. John Hayden (the driver) and his brother George were the owners of the business. The ice company was located on South Central Street with offices on South Main Street. Such ice wagons were a familiar sight in many neighborhoods until after World War II, when the electric refrigerator became an everyday appliance.

Dr. George Cogswell. Medical man, property owner, and president of the Trustees of Bradford Academy, Dr. Cogswell was Bradford's most renowned citizen in the second half of the nineteenth century. Note the splendid black marble fireplace, the classical prints on the wall, the oriental carpets, and the bell pull by his chair for summoning his servants.

The Parlor of Dr. Cogswell's House. This is the parlor of a very wealthy man. The heavily carved furniture was from Italy. In this room, each spring, he would entertain the faculty and the graduating class of Bradford Academy. Dr. Cogswell's portrait, now at Bradford College, hangs on the wall. In later years, this handsome building would become the clubrooms for generations of Boy Scouts and Girl Scouts of Sacred Hearts Parish.

The Cogswell House. This elegant Tuscan-style house, enlarged and modernized from its original Federal style, was at the corner of Main and Doane Streets. The name for Doane Street was taken from the family name of Cogswell's mother. The Cogswell House was razed in 1959 when Sacred Hearts School was expanded.

The Warren Ordway House. Directly opposite the Cogswell House stood the equally elegant, upper-class home of the Ordways, Haverhill shoe manufacturers. It is in an Italian Villa style with an elaborate Corinthian column stretching the height of the house at the main entrance. The house was moved around the corner to Carleton Avenue in 1908 where it became the rectory for the priests of Sacred Hearts Church.

Reverend John Graham. Graham was a Haverhill-born Catholic priest, and the first pastor of Sacred Hearts church. The church was built on the Ordway lot on the other side of an invisible line that separated the "Lower End" of Bradford, where the Irish and French-Canadian immigrants lived, from the "Yankee" homes on South Main Street, where the immigrants worked as servants.

Laying the Cornerstone at Sacred Hearts Church, 1910. After two years of construction, the church building was rapidly rising. While the church choir sings on the platform, priests and servers carry out the dedication. The assembled congregation offers a wonderful overview of 1910 fashions.

Two
The Bradford Common Area

A View of the West Side of South Main Street from the Steeple of the White Church. Some of the homes visible are, from the left: the Pearl, the Morse-Atwood, and the A. Ordway Houses. Behind the Ordway is the Franklin Engine House. Partially obscured by trees on the Common is the Kimball Tavern. To the right is the Albert Kimball House. Most noticeable is the great open space to the west of the houses on South Main Street reaching down to the riverside. The Greenleaf School and Bradford Town Hall would one day occupy most of the central open area.

The Brick Store. Built prior to 1820 by Moses Kimball, the tavern innkeeper, this structure was used as a store and shoe shop before becoming a dwelling. The house has since been razed and the space is now a parking lot for a funeral home.

Posing for the Camera. This group was photographed in front of the Brick Store and the home of Dr. Francis Anthony. Dr. Cogswell's house is visible to the far left.

The Dr. Francis Anthony House, 210 South Main Street at South Green Street. This Queen Anne-style dwelling was built in 1888. Dr. Anthony maintained his office here as well as his home. The building is now Farmer's Funeral Home.

The Frederick Johnson House, 191 South Main Street. Dating from the 1820s, this home was located next to the Warren Ordway House, where Sacred Hearts Church is today. Johnson (1789–1880) was a trader, the brother of Leonard, and the father of Abby, who was principal of Bradford Academy. In later years, the church acquired this property and used it for meeting rooms. The building was taken down to be replaced by a lawn.

Kimball Tavern. The oldest part of this house (the left front room when facing the front) dates from the 1690s. It acquired its present shape in the 1790s about the time it became a tavern. In 1803, a group of Bradford townspeople met in the Tavern Room (right front) to found Bradford Academy as a school of higher education for their children. Bradford College acquired the tavern in 1967 and restored it to its 1800 appearance. Jacob Kimball (1803–1869) and his family, the last of that name to live in the house, can be seen in this photograph.

The Ordway Double House, 239 South Main Street. This was built in 1831 as a commercial venture. The lower floors held a shoe shop and a general store, with living quarters on the upper floors. Alfred Ordway, Haverhill's premier shoe baron, bought the left half of the building in 1880 and lived in it until his death in 1922. The belvedere atop the house is an Italianate touch and must have been added to the Greek Revival house twenty or more years after its construction. South Elm Street is to the left of the lower picture.

The Morse-Atwood House, Corner of South Main and South Elm Streets. This abode was built by Isaac Morse between 1849 and 1851 and bought by Dr. George Atwood in 1895. South Elm Street, to the right, connects South Main Street to the railroad depot. The railroad reached Bradford in 1839. South Elm Street appears on Walling's 1854 map, but without any houses on it. Its presence would open up much of this west end of Bradford to development, and by the 1870s, it was lined with workingmen's cottages.

The Junction of South Main, South Elm, and Salem Streets. Dr. George Allen's new house is in the right rear of the photograph. The trolley line ran east along Salem Street and south along South Main Street. The "horseless carriage" to the left is a portent of the future when the trolley would become obsolete.

The Horatio Pearl House, 259 South Main Street. This classic Greek Revival structure was built by Isaac Morse in 1836 as a double house. The Pearl family, prominent in law and local politics, bought half the house in 1850, and later owned and occupied the entire house. The Pearls led the opposition to the annexation movement in the 1890s. In 1934, this house became the Bradford Branch Library. It is now an office building.

The Kimball-Durgin House, 267 South Main Street. A fine example of the Colonial Revival style that flourished at the turn of the century, this house was built in 1894 by George Kimball but was occupied for many years by the George Durgin family, who were Haverhill shoe manufacturers.

Pausing to Pose in the Snow. Two Academy girls stand beside the newly built Kimball-Durgin House, across from the Bradford Common. Kimball Tavern can be seen in the distance.

The Albert Laburton Kimball House. This classic French Empire-style house, with its characteristic mansard roof and paired windows, stood at the corner of South Main and Chadwick Streets. Mr. Kimball (1837–1889) is seated on the front steps. The house dates from the late 1860s. In later years, it served as a dormitory for the Academy. It was torn down in the 1970s and replaced by nondescript townhouses.

A Horse and Buggy Passing Bradford Common, 1890s.

The Merrill-Horne House, Corner of South Main and Chadwick Streets. This imposing example of the Second Empire style was built in 1865 by John F. Merrill but has belonged to the Horne family for many years. Paired with the Albert Kimball House on the opposite corner of Chadwick Street, and facing the equally impressive Farrar House and Carleton School on the other side of South Main Street, these four grand homes emphasized the significance of the Common area as the heart of old Bradford. This photograph is of recent vintage but the house is little changed from its 1890s appearance.

The White Church in the Snow, c. 1895. To the right of the church is the Samuel Hopkinson House, built between 1856 and 1859 in the Italian Villa style. It is the only house in the area to have retained its belvedere. Beyond the Hopkinson House is the Palfrey House, a Colonial Revival-style structure built about 1897.

Reverend John D. Kingsbury. The eleventh pastor of the White Church, Reverend Kingsbury served from 1866 to 1900. The road to West Boxford, variously known as Joel's Road and School Road, was renamed Kingsbury Avenue in his honor.

Two Carletonians at Bradford Academy. Young gentlemen from Carleton School visit three young ladies from neighboring Bradford Academy. Given the rules of the day, the visiting was most likely in the front parlor in the presence of a chaperone.

The Farrar House at 282 South Main Street and Carleton School at 286 South Main Street. Located on the south side of the Common, the Farrar House was built in 1894 in a flamboyant Queen Anne style. The earlier building to the right is a mid-century symmetrical Italian Villa-style house, built by William Kimball and intended to be "the finest house in Essex County." Professor Isaac Carleton conducted his School for Boys and Young Men here in the late 1800s (see cover image). In this photograph, the belvedere on the house is still intact.

The Arthur F. Durgin House, 7 Byron Street at Highland Avenue, 1919. This is one of a number of Queen Anne-style houses built on this street in the 1890s. Byron Street was one of the first new streets on the east side of South Main Street and the size and style of the houses indicate that Bradford was becoming a desirable housing choice for Haverhill's new generation of professionals and businessmen.

The House at 12 Byron Street under Construction. This building appears to have been built about 1895 for an electrical contractor, Herbert Kimball (son of Albert L. Kimball). It is unusual to find a photograph of the actual construction process. The African-American laborer sitting in the window frame is not identified but could possibly be Richard Broadnax, who lived with his two brothers at 28 South Elm Street.

View Toward Haverhill. This unique view was taken in the 1890s by an Academy student from a third-floor window. The White Church steeple pierces the sky. The bare hills of Haverhill are a reminder of how recently animal grazing and farming had been a part of the city's economy. The house in the foreground is at the corner of South Park and Highland Streets. It had been recently constructed when this photograph was taken.

Three
The East End

Bradford's Oldest Road, *c.* 1895. Salem Street, from Bradford Common through South Groveland, marks the path the original settlers trod as they moved inland from Rowley in the 1660s. The first church building and the original burial ground were on this road. The age and popularity of the street have made it a treasure of house architectural styles. In the photograph above, young children play with their pony and sleigh in front of the Walter Goodell House at 21 Salem Street, a Greek Revival structure built between 1853 and 1857, with some later Italianate trim added.

Trolley Tracks Run along Salem Street by the Common. The Common was established in 1751 when the third meetinghouse of the First Church of Christ was built. The previous two meetinghouses had been located further along Salem Street where the old burial ground is. This new location near the ferry to Haverhill suggests that the two towns on each side of the river were drawing closer to each other as early as the eighteenth century.

The Harrison Chadwick House, 8 Salem Street at South Chestnut Street, built 1836–37. This Greek Revival-style structure was built as a double house by shoe manufacturers George K. Montgomery and Humphrey Hoyt. It was bought by Harrison Chadwick, prominent businessman, politician, and orator, in 1865. Chadwick and his wife stand in front of the house.

The Eliphalet Kimball House. This home, originally at 16 Salem Street, now at 24 South Pine Street, dates from the end of the eighteenth century. It was built in a simplified Federal, or Adam, style, although an additional bay has been added to its right side upsetting the symmetry usually associated with this style of house. Kimball and his wife stand in front of the house.

Brooks and Elizabeth Palmer, c. 1910. The two children are playing with their miniature train outside their family home at 47 Salem Street, at the corner of Salem and Colby Streets. Brooks Palmer became a noted author and specialist on American clocks.

Captain Henry Walker and Son. A sea captain, Walker stood outside his home at 31 Salem Street with his son and dog for this portrait. The front-gable Greek Revival-style house is located next to where Hawthorne Street now turns off of Salem Street.

The Haseltine Family Monument in Elmwood Cemetery. The Haseltines were one of Bradford's most distinguished families—members were noted as educators and missionaries to foreign lands. The style of the monument and the design of this mid-century cemetery suggests that burial grounds had become memorial parks that honored rather than mourned the dead. This monument especially commemorates George Haseltine (1829–1915), an internationally known patent lawyer.

The Peabody School, *c.* 1910. Built in 1894, this school was named for the large and influential Peabody family, whose farmstead was on Salem Street near South Pine Street.

The House of George Kimball (1791–1862), 232 Salem Street. Built about the time of George's marriage in 1820, this brick, Federal-style house with a hipped roof bears a close resemblance to that built for George's brother David on 13 Ferry Street (p. 25). It was constructed with bricks from a brickyard at the river behind George's farm.

Shoveling Snow near Silsby's Farm, 1920. The farmhouse and barn in the background stand atop a gentle slope down to the Merrimack River, with what may well be one of the loveliest vistas in Bradford. The farm is located at 436 Salem Street near the junction with Old Groveland Road. Shoveling snow for the Public Works Department was laborious work but it brought decent, albeit irregular, wages for many young men until well into the mid-1900s.

A Winter's Sleigh Ride, February 26, 1910. Dashing through the snow . . . in a two-horse open pung! (A pung was a large sleigh.)

Skiing off Salem Street, 1900. This photograph indicates that this relatively new winter sport already had a following. The location is probably somewhere close to where the present Bradford Ski Area is.

Hikers at a Well, *c.* 1894. Academy girls pause on their walk. The house in the background is not identified, but it resembles the main building of Island Stock Farm, which was just beyond the Old Bradford Burial Ground.

A Candid 1892 Snapshot. "At 'Niagara Falls,' on Salem Street," reads the caption of this photograph from an Academy student's album. There is no further identification of the location but it could be one of the hills near Old Groveland Road.

A Wagon Ride into the Countryside, c. 1910. The riders may be *en route* to the Baldpate Inn in Georgetown—a favorite journey for Academy students.

Island Stock Farm, Salem Street, c. 1885. This model farm was owned by entrepreneur Henry Hale, son of philanthropist E.J.M. Hale. Thoroughbred horses were grazed on Porter's Island in the Merrimack River behind the farm. All of Hale's property was sold at auction in the early 1890s. The farm buildings still stand; the barns have been converted to houses, located on Salem Street near Maynard Avenue. Hale established the Bradford Aqueduct Company on the Island and had the artesian wells that provided Bradford's first public water supply dug.

The Island Park Golf Course, 1910. This area moved from model farm to water company to golf course in twenty short years. Though, technically, Porter's Island is on the Haverhill side of the old town line, it is physically closer to Bradford and thus rates inclusion in this volume.

Edith Howe, c. 1910. Howe, of Summer Street in Haverhill, tees off at the Island Park Golf Course.

Haverhill Viewed from Salem Street, *c.* 1894. This photograph was probably taken near Silsby's Farm at 436 Salem Street.

The East School on South Cross Road, off of Salem Street, 1916. This is a typical one-room schoolhouse constructed in the nineteenth century, with separate entrances for boys and girls.

The Horne Family Dairy, 666 Salem Street. Bradford and Haverhill had numerous small dairy operations. Horse-driven milk wagons could still be seen on local streets up until World War II. Charles Horne, owner of the dairy, stands by his wagon with members of his family to his right.

The Chadwick House, 460 Chadwick Road. Chadwick Road was part of a series of connected back roads that tied Salem Street at Bradford's east end to Boston Road in Ward Hill at Bradford's southwest corner. It was the direct route from West Bradford to the first meetinghouses. In this photograph, all the family members, and their laundry, make an appearance for the photographer. This house has since been razed.

Four

The West End

Bradford Depot. The 1839 decision to run the Boston & Maine Railroad far to the west of the main streets of Bradford and Haverhill eventually turned farmlands into residential areas and led to factories being built near the depots. In Bradford, this meant new streets and new populations. The area around the Bradford depot (shown here c. 1900) was home to Irish and Canadian immigrants, many of whom worked for the railroad or in Gilman's Hat Factory on Railroad Avenue. The railroad bridge across the Merrimack had a pedestrian walk, which allowed residents at this end of town to cross over to Haverhill to work in the shoe shops that proliferated there from the 1870s on.

The Greenleaf School. Named for famed educator and mathematician Benjamin Greenleaf, this school was erected in 1884. Bradford's town offices were also in this building, and the large auditorium was the setting for the town's famous raucous town meetings, as well as local entertainments. This photograph shows the South Elm Street side of the school looking down Chadwick Street

The People's Methodist Episcopal Church. This church, located near the Greenleaf School on Chadwick Street, was built in 1891. The original siding can be seen here, and shows the influence of both the shingle style and the stick style (exposed framing).

The Dr. Herbert Wales House, Corner of South Pleasant and Chadwick Streets. This is a lovely example of Italianate style with particularly decorative window details. Dr. Wales was a dentist with an office in Haverhill.

The Charles G. Locke House. This two-story brick house is at 177 South Pleasant Street, near the junction of South Elm, South Pleasant, and South Prospect Streets. A mason and builder, Mr. Locke began living here in 1892. Given his occupations, presumably he built the home. The bay window and front brackets on the door overhang are an Italianate touch on an otherwise plain face.

The Small Building at the Foot of Bradford Avenue on South Elm Street. This structure once served as a grocery store and a laundry. It is now a private home. The stairway on the side of the house leads to a metal door through which blocks of ice could be placed. The building to the left rear was an ice house. Michael Shugrue, the grocer, owned the house next door, which has his first store built into the lower level.

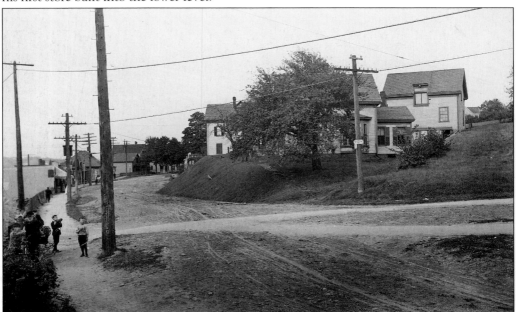

South Elm and Blossom Streets Meet Laurel Avenue at the Depot. This photograph was taken by W.P. Johnson. His young sons are on the left. Shugrue's Market is to the left rear, by the telephone pole.

Blossom Street before Re-Grading in 1906. "Doc" Lorenzo D. Sargent's pharmacy is at the foot of the street. The decision to build a new bridge across the Merrimack in 1906 meant that an underpass had to be created under the railroad tracks. This required the lowering of the three streets that met at that point. The houses along that part of Blossom, Locke (now Laurel), and South Elm Streets were left perched many feet above street level and accessible only by steep flights of stairs. The cement and granite walls used to buttress the hillsides are still in evidence on Laurel Avenue.

Blossom and Locke Streets after Re-Grading. Sargent's Pharmacy is gone, but neighborhood children were left with a splendid hilly street for wintertime sledding.

Michael Shugrue's Grocery Store, South Elm Street. The further end of this wooden building was occupied by Chin Fung, a Chinese laundryman who lived at the back of his shop. The Georgetown branch of the railroad ran directly behind this building. Immediately to the right is the stairway that led to the path under the Georgetown branch railroad tracks and onto the footwalk over the railroad bridge. The building is now a package store and social club.

Grocery Shopping, 1900. Dan Donovan, like many others, ran a monthly tab at Shugrue's. Steak, baked beans, and yeast for homemade bread were regular purchases in an age when beef was a staple of the diet and chicken was a luxury.

The Footwalk to the Railroad Bridge behind Shugrue's Market. This walk went under the Georgetown branch tracks and on to the walkway on the railroad bridge to Haverhill.

Footwalk to the Railroad Bridge. This time the walk is viewed from the railroad bridge with the houses along South Elm Street and Bradford Avenue in the background.

Off to a Picnic! A group of Academy girls dressed in their best traveling clothes and carrying picnic baskets prepare for a ride to the countryside from the Bradford train station.

At the Bradford Depot. Two neighborhood lads have an up close and personal look at a coal-fired steam engine.

The Great Train Wreck of 1888. On January 10, 1888, an express train from Boston on its way to Portland, Maine, derailed at the Bradford end of the bridge just beyond the junction with the Georgetown line. A car midway on the train left the track pulling the remaining cars with it. One of the cars crashed into a water tank alongside the tracks, pulling the tank down onto the car and crushing the tank house beneath it. More than a dozen passengers, and railroad workers who had been in the tank house warming up, were killed on the spot, or died of their injuries within the week.

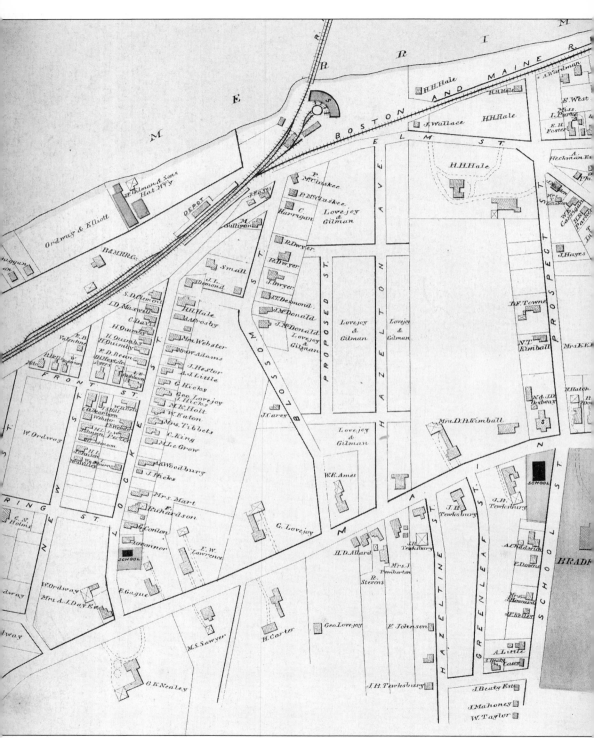

Bradford Village, 1884. The centrality of Bradford Academy, the clustering of the population in the area from the Common to the river, the new area of growth by the railroad depot, and the

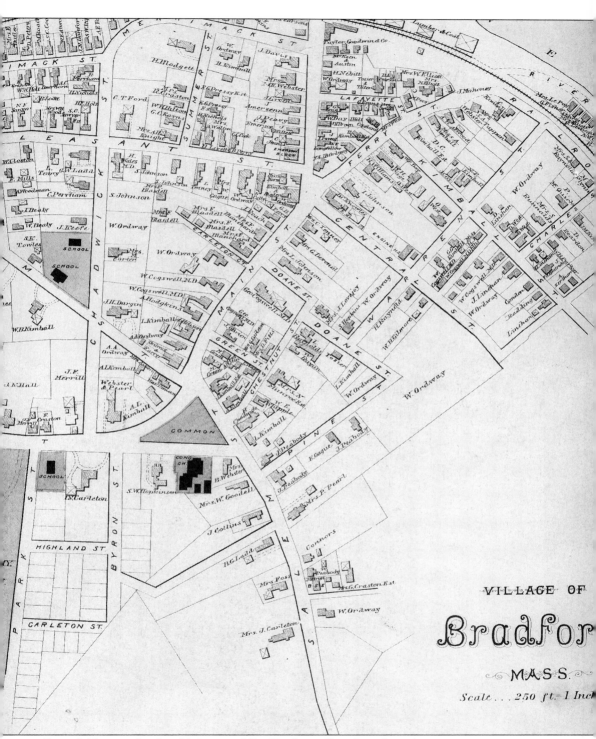

still-available open land in "downtown" Bradford are all evident from this map.

The 1888 Railroad Disaster. This photograph is from a postcard issued soon after the event. It bears the startling message, "Welcome!" Among those killed in the wreckage was sectionhand John Madden, of South Elm Street in Bradford. He left a young family including a son, Michael, who would graduate from Bradford High School and Holy Cross College, become a Catholic priest, and later serve as pastor of Sacred Hearts Church.

Five
Bradford Academy and Its Neighbors

Bradford Academy, now Bradford College, April 1915. High on a hill, and apart from the built-up section of town, the school commanded a grand vista. But the railroad, the trolley, and a burgeoning population brought the town to the Academy. By the beginning of the twentieth century, what had been just a scattering of farmhouses around the school had become a full-fledged neighborhood of modest-to-expensive single-family homes. Academy girls are shown here going through their exercises before a row of new houses on South Park Street.

Good Fences and Good Neighbors. This wrought-iron fence separated the Academy from its neighbors as the new construction continued. The house closest to the photographer is at the corner of South Park Street and Euclid Avenue.

South Park Street Looking toward South Main Street from Highland Street. Recently planted trees and a gas street lamp grace the new neighborhood.

The Dining Room of 4 South Park Street. This was the home of Matthew Scott, a commercial traveler, who moved here in 1905.

The Parlor of 4 South Park Street. The furniture here and in the dining room above is much less highly decorated than that previously shown for Dr. George Cogswell. In part, this reflects Mr. Scott's middle-class status, but also it reflects the impact of the simple Craftsman style of design popular at the end of the century.

Facing Academy Hall. These South Main Street homes are, from left to right: the Benjamin Greenleaf House at number 356; the Cogswell School; the Hatch House at number 333; and the Downes House at number 329, built between 1834 and 1841 for William Kimball and bought in 1850 by Benjamin Downes, a music teacher at the Academy.

The Hatch House. This home was built in the 1840s in a Greek Revival style for Rebecca Haseltine Emerson of the illustrious Haseltine clan. The Hatch family acquired the house in 1857 and occupied it until the death of Mary Hatch, a beloved public school teacher, in 1939. In later years it was a Bradford Junior College dormitory and it is now a private home.

Early Bradford Academy Buildings. This mid-nineteenth-century sketch shows the original 1803 building at the far left. "New Hall," in use from 1841 to 1869, is at the front left. After Academy Hall was built in 1869, New Hall was turned over to the town of Bradford to be used as a high school. The home of Benjamin Greenleaf, former master of the Academy, is partially visible in the center behind the trees. The Academy boarding house is on the right, where the Cogswell School now stands.

View of Bradford High School beyond Academy Hall Drive. After annexation, the high school (on the left in this photograph) continued to use this structure until the new Haverhill High School was completed in 1908. For a few more years, the fifth grade of the Cogswell School attended classes here. The old building was razed and the lot is now occupied by the Louis Hamel House, built in 1929.

The 1892 Bradford High School Football Team. Michael Madden, whose father, John Madden, was killed in the 1888 railroad disaster, is furthest to the right in the middle row.

The High School and the Benjamin Greenleaf House. The Greenleaf House was built in 1821, at the time of Greenleaf's marriage to Lucretia Kimball, in the Federal, or Adam, style—the almost-national design that could be found along the entire Atlantic coast in the decades after independence.

South Main Street at Haseltine Street. This view looks north to the Haseltine and Greenleaf Houses. Those families are now commemorated in the names of the side streets which cut through what was once those families' farmlands. The Haseltine House has been moved to Greenleaf Street, but the two other houses shown are still on their original sites.

A Home on Haseltine Street. The kitchen ell of this house is believed to be half of Willow Hall, the original Academy Building that once stood on Kingsbury Avenue (p. 71).

Kingsbury Avenue Houses, mid-1890s. The view from these homes overlooks man-made Lake Tupelo, shown here being enjoyed by canoeing students.

James Campbell Playing His Violin. This image was taken from a student photograph album dated 1893–95.

Everyone Loves a Baby! And student Frances Wood was no exception. Her 1893–95 photograph album contains these and other candid shots of neighborhood children. The baby carriage, the child's clothing, and the toys are rare glimpses into everyday life that would be difficult to recapture were it not for the camera and a young student's fondness for children.

Young Neighborhood Boys with a Bicycle and Dog. This is another *c*. 1893 photograph by Frances Wood.

The Cogswell School Basketball Team, 1904–1905. The students are, from left to right: (front row) Davis, the left guard; Barker, the captain and center; and Tirell, the left forward; (back row) Gillen, the manager and right guard; Dugdale, the right forward; and Cogswell, the substitute.

The Dr. George Cogswell School. This educational institution was built in 1891 on the site of the old Academy Boarding House in a Romanesque style made popular by architect Henry Hobson Richardson of Boston.

Dr. George Cogswell. Dr. Cogswell was a medical man, educator, land owner, and leader in all aspects of his life in Bradford for over three quarters of the nineteenth century. He began his practice of medicine in the town in 1830 and lived until 1901.

Daniel B. Kimball (1807–1879) of 367 South Main Street. Kimball was in the shoe findings business in Boston, but also listed himself as a "farmer."

The Daniel B. Kimball House. This home was built in 1846 for Jesse Kimball, who died before it was completed. It was built in the Greek Revival style with Egyptian Revival columns resembling lotus blossoms at the front entrance. From 1851 to 1856, the building served as a rent-free house for Academy girls who could not otherwise afford to attend the school. Daniel and Charlotte Tenney Kimball bought the property in 1856 and their family lived there until the 1940s. The house is now the Haverhill Day Nursery. Chandler Street and Leroy Avenue were carved out of the Kimball estate.

The John Howard House, 353 South Main Street. This California Spanish-style house with its handsome tile roof was built in 1917 by John F. Howard, the "mayonnaise king," who had made a fortune producing salad dressing. He began his business in the barn behind his house on 21 Kingsbury Avenue, but later moved the operation to the Island Park industrial complex.

The Original Lennox House, 378 South Main Street. George W. Lennox, a Haverhill leather manufacturer, built this fine Queen Anne-style house with mock Tudor details in 1890 on the site of the old Haseltine family house. Less than a decade later, Lennox's business partner, Charles Briggs, built his own home (visible to the left) on the next corner, 364 South Main Street, in a Colonial Revival, or neo-Georgian, style. Not to be outdone, Lennox greatly enlarged his still-new house and put on the neo-Georgian facade that remains. The house has been a nursing home in recent years and currently is used by Bradford College for offices.

George Lovejoy House, 389 South Main Street. This is a classic Greek Temple house with Ionic columns. Lovejoy, a wool merchant with offices in Boston, owned much of the land between the Daniel Kimball estate and Blossom Street. Lovejoy Street is named for him. At the time of the annexation issue, Freeman Small, a carpenter and annexation proponent, lived here. The facade has since been altered, with the Ionic capitals removed and a second-floor porch added. The house is now a realtor's office.

Professor William H. Goodyear. An art historian and visiting lecturer at Bradford Academy in the late 1890s, Professor Goodyear strolls along South Main Street, the epitome of the well-dressed professional man.

Lake Tupelo. The western end of this man-made pond was completed in 1872 as a "skating rink." The water that filled it was pumped up from the Merrimack River by a pumping station at the foot of South Prospect Street. In its expanded form, with its lovely arched bridge, it provided a tranquil spot of beauty for both the residents of the school and for its neighbors.

Academy Hall with Students, 1888. The original small entry porch shown here was changed in 1916 to the more imposing one that stands today. The student body averaged about 150 students in the 1880s and 1890s, most of them in residence, along with their teachers, all in this one building, which also contained their classrooms, dining room, library, and gymnasium.

Academy Students in front of Academy Hall, 1888. It is difficult to realize that these young women, attired as they are in their fashionable dresses and hats, are only teenagers. Certainly, the young woman in the second row with the lorgnette is trying her hardest to look sophisticated.

A Dormitory Room, c. 1890. Girls lived in three-room suites designed for two students, but with the growing popularity of the school, there would often be three or four girls per suite, until the west wing (1884) and the east wing (1892) were added to Academy Hall to alleviate crowding.

A Banquet in a Dormitory Room, c. 1895. The light dresses and the abundance of flowers suggests that this is an end-of-the-year party.

"A Break from Studying—Helen Brown's Birthday," 1901. We rarely have a chance to see the intimate side of life one hundred years ago. Young ladies would never appear in their nightgowns and wrappers in public, but a friend with a camera was an exception and we are left with this delightful picture of a late-night revel.

The Mandolin Club and One Guitar, Roof of Academy Hall, c. 1901. The roof is now off-limits, but for many years it was a favorite spot for students to gather, as many surviving photographs make clear.

Professor Samuel M. Downs. Professor Downs, a professor of music for over thirty years at the Academy, instructs a student at the piano.

"Tennis Anyone?", 1888. How did they ever play in those outfits?

The Tennis Courts by Lake Tupelo near Kingsbury Avenue. The courts were in this location until they had to be moved to the back field to allow the construction of the library and Conover Hall.

More Appropriate Tennis Garb, 1890s. These outfits seem better suited for tennis than the 1888 costumes on the previous page.

A Bicycle Built for One. Off for a spin on the Academy's sweeping front drive.

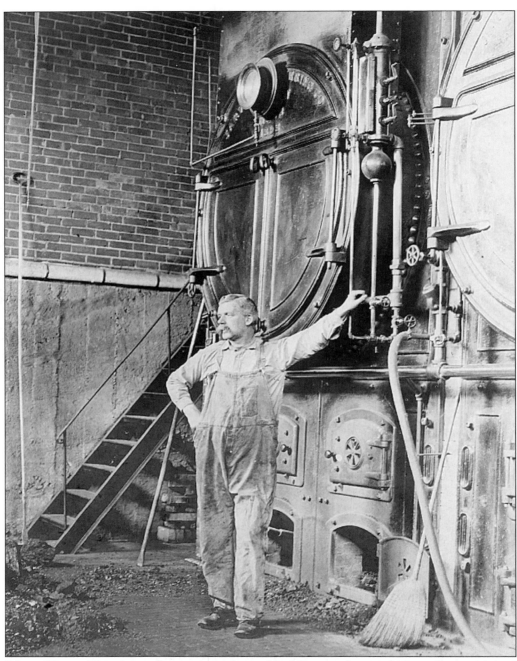

Edwin Elliott. This man was superintendent of buildings and grounds from the opening of Academy Hall in 1870 until 1902. His mother had been in charge of the boarding house that preceded Academy Hall and she moved with Edwin and his family into a suite of rooms on the first floor of the Academy, where they resided for the next thirty years. Elliott's wife, Mary, was a teacher at the Cogswell School for many years. His son Charles, later the chief engineer of the Haverhill Electric Company, was given the middle name of "Bradford" as a reminder of his birth at the Academy.

"Our Dennis, The Mailman." Dennis Reardon immigrated from Ireland, and by 1870 he was employed at Bradford Academy. An early Academy history refers to him with ethnic stereotyping as "lazy, good-natured . . . [whose] only other duty . . . [except] trunk lifting was carrying the mail bag three times daily to and from the post office." Yet, there are over a half-dozen copies of this picture in the College's archives, suggesting the fondness graduates had for him.

Dennis Reardon at Work. Obviously, Dennis did more than lift trunks and carry mail, as the above demonstrates. Bradford Academy and the well-to-do families of Bradford hired their domestic staff from among the Irish immigrant community. Though Dennis is listed in the 1900 census as being unable to read or write, he had owned a home in the Lower End since 1878. After his years at the Academy, he became the janitor at the South Kimball Street School near his home.

"Posing." The sub-title of this image is, "An Evening of Robert Burns Poetry, April 26, 1902." It provides the viewer with a sense of how young ladies, away from home, surrounded themselves with mementos of family and friends.

The 1904 Republican Convention, Student-Style. These students staged a mock convention, complete with a mock elephant, Uncle Sam, and a Teddy Roosevelt look-alike. The location is the second-floor hallway of Academy Hall.

Skating on Lake Tupelo, 1911. Skating was enjoyed by both students and neighborhood children alike. Because of its shallowness, the lake has always been a "safe" area, ready for skating and ice hockey games long before larger bodies of water are.

Girls' Basketball. This sport has brought many championships to Haverhill in recent decades. This 1904 photograph suggests some worthy ancestors for today's players, especially the young lady diving for the ball in the foreground. But today's players never had to contend with long skirts and grass-covered courts!

A Decorous Game of Field Hockey, early 1890s. The younger students are in middy blouses and bloomers, while the older students attempt to engage in this active sport in their ground-length skirts. Ah! the price of female fashion!!

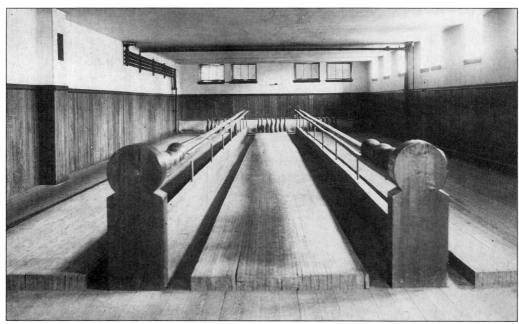

Bowling Lanes in the Ground Floor of Academy Hall. In an attempt to add more physical activity into the students' curriculum before the gymnasium was built, these bowling lanes were put into the new west wing, completed in 1884. All that remain are traces of the very narrow boards used in the lanes, now hidden away in a basement office.

A Toboggan Slide, Back Campus, from a 1900 Photograph Album. As another means of providing athletic activity within the confines of the school grounds, the Academy put up this toboggan run. The slide is off to the left and the three students, impatient for some snow, sit on the double-channeled ascent, one channel for the stairway and the other for the toboggan.

A Giant Snow Roller, from a 1900 Photograph Album. Rather than shovel or plow snow, rollers would be used to pack it down, enabling sleighs to move easily. Rollers were also used to create cross-country ski trails across the back campus.

Bradford's New Gymnasium, Opened in February 1904. For the previous twenty years, the first floor of the west wing (where the president's office is now) had served as a very narrow and confined gym.

An Early Form of Billboard for Haverhill's "The People's House Furnishing Co." Two Academy girls clown for the photographer during their daily walk in the countryside.

Sail to Salisbury Beach on the Steamer *City of Haverhill*, October 1891. The students provided their own entertainment with banjos. The boat ride down the Merrimack River to the Atlantic Ocean was a much-anticipated treat for students and townspeople alike for many years until the advent of the automobile.

Wading in the Surf, Salisbury Beach, Massachusetts, 1893. The raised skirts may have bared an unusual amount of flesh for the standards of the day, but the girls kept their hats and coats on!

Academy Hall. The hall, built 1869–70 on "Chadwick's Meadow," is shown here before extensive landscaping changed its bare appearance. This early photograph gives a good sense of how imposing this building must have been, situated as it was, high on a hill with only open space around it.

Sleigh Ride to Andover, c. 1893. The girls, with their Bradford pennant, are probably on their way to Abbot Academy or Phillips Academy for a social. Whatever the reason, it appears to be a delightful way to spend a winter's day.

Six

The Upper End

A Gathering of Prominent Haverhill Men. Beyond the Academy and its immediate neighborhood, there was little of the concentrated population that marked the Lower End. Only Laurel Avenue had any significant number of houses. All else along the road to Andover was either old farmhouses or large, elegant estates inhabited principally by Haverhill businessmen. One such estate was that of Edward Hammond Hoyt, whose house stood where the Bradford Firehouse and the entrance to Caleb Dustin Hunking School are now, opposite Laurel Avenue. On August 1911, Hoyt hosted this distinguished gathering of prominent Haverhill shoe manufacturers and lawyers. From left to right are: (standing) Edward Hoyt, Charles W. Arnold, J. Otis Carleton, Associate Supreme Court Justice and Haverhill resident William G. Moody, and Hazen B. Goodrich; (seated) Dana T. Dudley, an unidentified man, and E.G. Frothingham.

The Robert and Olive Stevens Farm, 1879. This small farm was in marked contrast to the luxury of Hoyt's house. It stood on South Main Street between today's Lamoille and Lexington Avenues. The house was still standing at the turn of the century, but Olive lived there alone as a widow.

Judge Henry Carter's Home. After moving here from Maine in 1856, Carter had this house built for himself. It is a rare Gothic Revival-style house, midway between the Stevens farm and the Hoyt estate, at what would become Fernwood Avenue. Carter was judge of the Police Court in Haverhill. The Gothic Revival style was not as popular for domestic architecture as was the Italianate or Greek Revival. Judge Carter died in 1898, soon after annexation.

An Italianate-Style House, Dating from 1851–55. This building faces Judge Carter's house across South Main Street. Mrs. Martha Howe, a widow and paper box manufacturer, lived here in the 1890s. In the twentieth century, this was the home of Lewis Hovey, publisher of the *Haverhill Record*.

A Four Square Colonial Revival House. The first decade of the twentieth century saw an explosion of building and the creation of new streets in Bradford, especially in the upper end beyond the Academy, and off of Salem Street near the Elmwood Cemetery. This style house with its hipped roof was so popular that newcomers to town took to referring to it as the "Haverhill house." Lexington Avenue had recently been developed when this particular house was built.

Atop Libby's Hill. For decades, a favorite hike was up Libby's Hill. The footpath to the top began in the fields behind "Teddy" Hoyt's house. From its summit, Chadwick's Pond was visible, as can be seen here. Today, widespread development off of Kingsbury Avenue, and the Presidential Gardens and Forest Acres developments off of South Main Street, have obliterated any sense of the "escape to the country" that a few hours on Libby's Hill could give.

A Trolley on Locke Street, now Laurel Avenue. To the left is the Locke Street primary school, once the vestry for the "White Church" (p. 2). It is now a private home. To the center and right are the Ingersoll and White Houses. The White House had just been completed. The trolley line ended half way down Laurel Avenue. The "turn-around" is still visible in a large, flat area of open land.

Daniel and Mary Donovan, Recent Irish Immigrants, Married November 1890. Within a year the couple had bought a seven-room cottage on Locke Street. Dan was a laborer whose life was a far cry from that of "Teddy" Hoyt and his friends, yet their houses were less than 100 yards apart.

The Caterer's Bill for Dan and Mary Donovan's Wedding Party. H.C. Tanner was Haverhill's leading caterer. The modest repast of cakes, pies, and cream breads, plus 3 pounds of candy, cost $9.68, a pittance today, but a week's wages for a laboring man in the 1890s.

Odd Fellows' Building, 24 Main Street.

Haverhill, Mass., Nov 5th 1890

Mr D Donovan #30 Elm St.

BOUGHT OF H. C. TANNER,

Caterer and Confectioner.   Ice Creams of the Finest Quality.

Catering for Large and Small Parties, Wedding Receptions, etc., at short notice.

	2	Wedding Cakes		4.50	
	12	Washington Pies		96	
	2	Sheets White Mountain Cake		50	
	6	" Sponge "		72	
	3	" Centennial "		36	
	10	Loaves Large Cream Bread		80	
	15	" Small " "		60	
Nov. 6	8	" Large " "		64	
"	3	Lbs Candy		60	$9.68

Paid

The R.L. Wood School. This school was built in 1906 and named for incumbent mayor Roswell Wood, who in his inaugural address that year had decried school department expenses! This was one of four city schools, designed in the same style by noted architect C. Willis Damon. The school and its large playground have been a center for neighborhood activities since its construction.

A Birthday Party, Wood School Neighborhood, c. 1910. The little boy in the center row was the honoree. The two little girls to the right in the front row are Marion and Helen McCarthy.

Helen McCarthy. Helen poses for what was intended to be her last picture. Because she had become seriously ill and her life was feared for, it was decided to take one last photograph of little Helen—a not uncommon use of photography at the time. The photograph was unnecessary. Helen McCarthy Bryant recently celebrated her ninetieth birthday!

Seven-Year-Old Agnes and Three-Year-Old Marion Donovan, 1900. The children of Dan and Mary stand on the front steps of their house on Laurel Avenue. Mary, their mother, died in September of that year from a severe form of consumption.

Daniel Harold Donovan, c. 1909. A son from Dan's second marriage, Daniel represents the height of children's fashion in his sailor suit.

Jack Donovan's Wagon. Jack lived at the corner of Front Street and High Street (now Germain Avenue), at the end of the Wood School playground. He was a teamster for the Atherton-Byard Furniture Co. of Haverhill. His wagon is stopped at 2 Front Street, near the Laurel Avenue home of his uncle Dan.

Bathing Beauties at Old Orchard Beach, Maine. Marion Donovan, nineteen years after her previous picture (p. 104), had just been chosen "Miss Haverhill." Her best friend, shown in a daring swim attire of bare legs and bare arms, was Margaret R. Noonan, who in later years would become a most proper and dignified Bradford funeral director with a home and business on Salem Street.

The Outer Limits of Bradford Village. A trolley to Ward Hill pauses at South Main Street and Cumberland Avenue. The graceful stucco house on the left and the Craftsman-style homes on the right still stand, but the small pond where the children are playing has been filled in with newer houses.

Seven

Ward Hill

Ward Hill, One of Bradford's Oldest Areas. Early settlers established their farms here in the late seventeenth century. The area is located in the most southerly section of the town, adjacent to North Andover. Its most significant physical features are the great curving "neck" of land which produces a big bend in the Merrimack River, and the large hill which gives the area its name. More than 3 miles separate downtown Bradford from Ward Hill, with scattered settlement in between. This distance was diminished when the railroad came through and it was decided to establish a depot at Cross Road. Soon the area around the depot became the preferred location for a number of small "ten-footer" shoe shops.

Easing the Curve at Dead Man's Corner. Workers with picks and shovels laboriously chip away at the stone mound near "Haseltine's Corner." This area is adjacent to Alton Avenue and just south of the Cove Road underpass and Academy Lanes. Note the trolley tracks.

The Carleton House. This structure is located at 839 South Main Street, at "Haseltine's Corner," where South Main Street and Boston Road meet Ferry Road in Ward Hill. The house, whose framing beams came from a Methuen meetinghouse, was probably built in 1796. It is the only house of this type (center-chimney, hipped roof) in Bradford. It has been a restaurant and a veterinarian's office in recent years.

The Gage Day House, 872 Boston Road. Day (1811–1859) had been living at his grandfather Carleton's house at 839 South Main Street when he began plans to build a new house around the corner on Boston Road. He died after completing the barn only. His widow completed the building of this house in 1861. It has both Greek Revival and Italianate design features. Cedarland is now on this site.

Thomas McDonald's Farm, 920 Boston Road. The McDonalds were Irish immigrants who arrived in Bradford in the 1840s. Their son William became a lawyer, and their grandson Clifford, a judge. The house was taken down and rebuilt in Glastonbury, Connecticut, in 1973. The land is now a parking lot for Cedardale.

The Charles Phillips House, Willow Avenue. Phillips bought this eighteenth-century post-and-beam house when he returned from the Civil War. He had been wounded at the Battle of Gettysburg. His farm was located on what is officially known as Willow Avenue, but neighborhood children still call it by the name found on old maps: "Skunk Hill Road." Shown here are Phillips, his wife, her mother, and one of his sons with the family's horse.

Mrs. Page. "Grammy Page At 99" is the caption on this photograph. Mrs. Page, the mother-in-law of Charles Phillips, still had keen eyesight and all her "faculties" as she approached the century mark.

The T. William Thornton House, Willow Avenue. Willy Thornton married his neighbor, Ella Phillips (daughter of Charles), and they built this house in the 1890s. Willy's father, William Thornton, raised beef cattle and had an abattoir attached to his barn and a meat market in Haverhill. Willy, shown here with his wife and first two children, was a salesman.

Harry, Marion, and Ralph Thornton (Willy and Ella's Children), c. 1900. The boys are sporting their new summer haircuts.

The Thornton Family, October 1908. Two more sons have been added to the family, Charles and Willis, in the back row.

A First Period House, 989 Boston Road at the Junction with Willow Avenue and Oxford Avenue. This house was built in the 1700s in a simple, center chimney, First Period style. Its fields were incorporated into the new streets created by William Knipe in 1892. The north-facing front door, which runs counter to the tradition that houses be south-facing to take advantage of the sun, probably dates from that same date since the owners would probably have preferred to face the junction of streets created with Oxford Avenue.

A Ward Hill Baseball Team. The team members pose in the early twentieth century outside the West Bradford (or Ward Hill) school.

The Hiram Day House, 1226 Boston Road. This abode is considered to be the fourth house built in Bradford. The oldest portion is the right, or south-facing, side. Hiram, who took over the house and farm in 1855, was the fifth generation of his family to live here. The expansion of Route 125 in 1961 to allow for a connector road to I-495 required that the house be moved back off its original foundation about 30 feet. In 1971, the remaining farmland was sold to create the Farrwood Drive houses. The house remained in the Day family until 1977.

The West Bradford (or Ward Hill) School. This center for education was located at Haseltine's corner and then moved to Oxford Avenue in the 1890s when that area was developed by William Knipe. When a new brick school was built in 1915 (the Knipe School), the old building was moved to the rear of the schoolyard where it served as a community clubhouse until the 1970s. It has since been razed.

Ward Hill School Students at the Turn of the Century. The group includes a number of Thornton and Day children.

The Day-Prescott House, Ferry Road at Cross Street, Ward Hill. Generations of Days lived here as farmers and shoemakers. Benjamin Prescott, a farmer and leather cutter, joined the household in 1874, possibly through marriage. The house was razed to make room for the I-495 Connector Road.

The Nathan Kimball House, 130 Neck Road. This home was built about the time of Nathan's marriage in 1750. Samuel Kimball, last of his family to live here, sold the house to Randolph Rogers in 1902. Rogers was recuperating from a railroad accident and hoped to create a self-sufficient home. He succeeded. The third and fourth generations of the Rogers family operate Spring Hill Farm from the old homestead today.

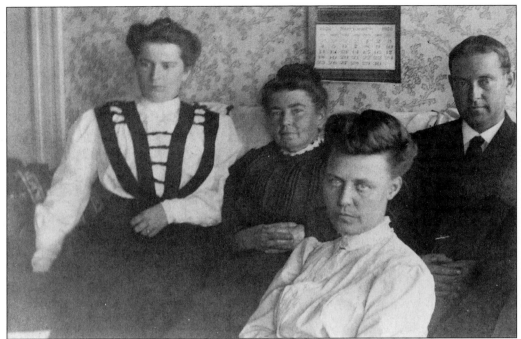

The Transformation of the Old Rural Ward Hill, 1890s. William Knipe, an English immigrant, was burned out of downtown Haverhill in the 1888 Great Fire. He decided to rebuild at the edge of town by the railroad station in Ward Hill. His new, large factory brought a change in both the society and economy of the area. Henry E. Day, the grandson of Hiram, is shown here with his family in 1906. Henry was a heel cutter, a highly skilled craft. His Queen Anne-style house on Ferry Road was quite unlike the simple farmhouses shown previously.

Middle Class Style at the Turn of the Century. The Christmas tree in the bay window and the upright piano are both from the Henry E. Day House. The tree, though scraggly, has the requisite doll perched in front. The piano, complete with family photographs, was the heart of domestic entertainment, and piano lessons were part of any ambitious person's proper education.

The Knipe Shoe Factory, Ward Hill. Shoe workers from the neighborhood head to work. William Knipe built more than a factory: he created an industrial village with new streets, architect-designed houses for his managers, "four-square" houses for his workers with families, and boarding houses for his unmarried workers. He owned all the properties and was renowned for turning over deeds of houses to loyal workers. Knipe even provided a private sewer system, and donated the land and helped fund the construction of the village church (below) about 1892. In gratitude, the new brick school in the village, built in 1916, was named in his honor.

Ruins of the Buena Vista Hotel. As part of the transformation of Ward Hill, a grand new hotel was built high atop of Head (or Ward) Hill. The building was completed in February 1891, then disaster struck. A severe nor-easter, possibly a tornado, ripped up the river valley and damaged the building beyond repair on the night of April 3, 1891.

The Second Buena Vista Hotel, Opened in May 1893. This was the highest structure in Essex County and was surmounted by a 72-foot observation tower that contained an 18-by-40-foot room for dinner parties. This photograph, taken from the Haverhill side of the Merrimack River, demonstrates how markedly the hotel stood out on the landscape.

The Buena Vista in Its Prime, *c.* 1896. Though successful for a while, this hotel never realized its promise. Its creators had envisioned an accompanying housing development on the Ward Hill Neck, serviced by an innovative monorail train from Lawrence to Haverhill. The train was not funded, so the house lots were not sold, and the hotel found itself competing for customers with the developing ocean front resorts. It was razed in 1910.

Haverhill Commandery of Knights Templar, a Masonic Organization, at the Rebuilt Buena Vista Hotel. Shoe manufacturer Alden Potter Jacques is the bearded man with the black hat and chesterfield coat, seated to the left at the side of the wagon.

Eight

Annexation

FACTS AND FIGURES

NOT SENTIMENT,

IN REGARD TO THE

Annexation of Haverhill and

Bradford.

Amount Saved on Taxes and Water Rents
to a Family of Five in Bradford, by
Annexation with Haverhill.

Taxes (assessed value House and Land
$2500)   7.40

Water Rent (including Bath Tub, Water
Closet and Hose)   4.85
                                        _____

Amount saved in these two items, $12.25

PRESS OF CHASE BROS., HAVERHILL, MASS.

A Pamphlet for Annexation. Annexation had been a political issue in Bradford and Haverhill since the latter became a city in 1870. Three times the issue was voted on, and three times it failed. If Bradford favored it, Haverhill did not, and vice versa. The final drive in 1896 was successful. Citizens and "other owners of real estate" in Bradford presented a petition to the General Court in Boston requesting a vote be taken on annexation. The petition was approved and the propaganda began. The financial arguments, as in the pamphlet shown above, stressed that a large municipality would be more economical, more attuned to the "progressive" demands of the age.

Oxford Avenue and the Knipe Shoe Factory. The first three names on the annexation petition were shoemen William and Mark Knipe, and their chief financier, William Smiley. (The streets in Ward Hill village spell out W.H. Smiley's name.) William Knipe had provided many services to the new residents of his village, but he could not, or would not, provide such newly popular municipal services as sidewalks and water systems. Funds for services to such a remote part of the town were repeatedly voted down at Bradford town meetings. If Bradford would not provide the services, Haverhill would.

Municipally Provided Water. In the 1890s, a municipal water system was in great demand. The Bradford Pumping Station was erected at great expense to the town in 1895 by the Bradford Aqueduct Company. Ward Hill wanted its share of the water but the town would not extend its pipes that far from the center of Bradford.

Constructing the New Bradford Reservoir. As the price for annexation, the City of Haverhill had to cover the costs of this new reservoir, which was completed in 1913.

"At The Crossroads." This photograph was taken about the time of the final annexation controversy. Bradford was indeed at a crossroads as it debated continued independence or annexation to Haverhill.

Bradford, Mass., August 1, 1896.

Page *17*   Line *2*   Residence *32 Locke*

Daniel Donovan

CHAP. 2, SEC. 47, G. ST. "No abatement shall be allowed to a person unless he makes application therefor within six months after the date of his tax bill."

The assessors will be in session at their office, Town Hall, Tuesday evening, Sept. 8th, Wednesday evening, Sept. 9th, from 7 until 9 o'clock, and Thursday afternoon, Sept. 10th, from 2 until 5 o'clock, to hear claims for abatements.

EDWARD E. BRADBURY,
CHARLES HASELTINE,   } Assessors.
NORMAN S. COLE,

At the annual town meeting held in March, 1896, the following vote was passed:

Voted, "That the Tax Bills shall be dated August 1st and due November 1st. Interest at the rate of 6 per cent per annum shall be allowed upon all taxes paid previous to November 1st, and upon all taxes not paid at that time, interest at the same rate shall be charged until paid." All taxes not paid January 1st, 1897, shall be immediately collected.

Also that a list of all persons whose taxes remain unpaid at the end of the year, the amount due, and the reason for non-payment, shall be printed in the Town Report.

In accordance with the above vote of the town, the collector will issue a summons, Jan. 1st, 1897, to all persons owing a tax on that date, for which a charge of twenty cents additional will be made.

WILLIAM A. KIMBALL,
Collector of Taxes.
Bradford, Aug. 1st, 1896.

Your Town, County and State Tax for 1896 is:

On POLL,	$2 00
PERSONAL ESTATE,	
REAL ESTATE,	24 70
TOTAL TAX,	
STREET WATERING, 1895,	
TOTAL,	26 70
INTEREST, { Six per cent per annum after Nov. 1st. }	
DEDUCTION, { For payment previous to Nov. 1st }	
COST,	
	26 70

1896 COLLECTOR'S OFFICE, DEC 10 1896 BRADFORD, MASS.

Received Payment,

William A. Kimball
Collector of Taxes.

Rate, $19.76 per $1000.   CHASE BROS., PRINTERS.

Office Hours—Monday, 9.30 to 12, 2 to 5 and 7 to 9; Tuesday, Wednesday, Thursday and Friday, 9.30 to 12, 2 to 5; Saturday, 9.30 to 12, 2 to 4 and 6 to 8.

A Final Tax Bill. Dan Donovan of Locke Street (Laurel Avenue) paid his taxes on December 10, 1896, midway between the date of the vote that approved annexation and the first day of the new year, 1897, when Bradford officially became Haverhill's seventh ward.

The New Faces of Ward Hill. Foremen, shoe cutters, and shoe workers at Knipe's Factory interrupt their baseball game to pose for the photographer. They represent the newcomers to town who were the main supporters of annexation. Of the eighteen names on the petition that brought this movement to a successful conclusion, the overwhelming majority were newcomers to Bradford, businessmen (especially in shoes and leather), or professional men. Except for the Knipes, most of these men had businesses in Haverhill and homes in Bradford. Other issues played a part, of course, but the lack of ties with Bradford's long past may have been the ultimate reason why the newcomers overwhelmingly chose annexation to independence.

GRADUATING EXERCISES

Class of '97

BRADFORD HIGH SCHOOL

Town Hall, Thursday Evening, June 24,

8 O'CLOCK.

Bradford High School Graduation, 1897. These students entered their senior year as residents of Bradford and graduated nine months later as residents of Haverhill. Students would continue to attend the old Bradford High School until 1908, when Haverhill's new high school was built, but, as in 1897, their diplomas would be signed by Haverhill's mayor, not Bradford's selectmen.

CLASS OF '97.

‡GENEVA MADELINE CONNOR.

*ALICE MARIA DAY.

*HARRY FOREST HADDOCK.

‡ETTA MYRTIE JUDKINS.

*HOWARD SEWELL LAKIN.

†ALICE JOSEPHINE McDONALD.

‡ANNIE GLIDDEN MORSE.

*ANNIE LOUISE PEABODY.

‡MARY EMMA PETERS.

†NELLIE JOSEPHINE PETERS.

*ARTHUR PAGE PHILLIPS.

*HELENA WINNIFRED REARDON.

*RICHMOND GROUT ROBERTS.

*FRANK FREELAND TYLER.

*General Course.   †English Course.   ‡Certificate for Partial Course.

The 1896 Bradford High School Football Team. This teams was the last to represent the independent town. The players, from left to right, are: (front row) George Norton, Theodore Bly, Fred Snelling, and Chris Glycart; (middle row) Ernest Peabody, Allan Alexander, Eddie Ring, William Kerrigan, and Fred Wiggin; (back row) Howard Howe, George Evans, James Gage, James (Jack) Morrison, and David Tilton. As part of the annexation agreement Bradford kept its library, its post office, its high school (for another decade)—and its name! As long as its name endures, so shall some fragment of its independence survive.

OBITUARY

Mother Bradford died suddenly from an overdose of damphoolishness at midnight on Nov. 3, aged 225 years. She left a will bequeathing all her vast domains to her big sister across the river. Being of unsound mind, the will may be contested. The burial will take place on January 1. Kind friends will please send forget-me-nots.

Grand old Bradford, thou hast left us,
And our loss we deeply feel,
But 'tis fools which hast bereft us.
How we will laugh to hear them squeal.

—A MOURNER
Bradford, Nov. 5

On November 5, 1896, two days after the vote for annexation passed, this notice appeared in the Haverhill newspapers. It was surrounded by a black border.